Finding Home

FINDING HOME

A Spiritual Journey of
Self-Discovery through Poetry

NOELLE PETERSON

All rights reserved. No part of this publication may be reproduced, distributed, or transmitted in any form by any means, including photocopying, recording, or other electronic methods without the prior written permission of the author, except in the case of brief quotations embodied in reviews and certain other noncommercial uses permitted by copyright law. For permission requests, write to the author at the email address below.

noellethepoet@gmail.com
http://noelle-peterson.com

Copyright © 2024 Noelle Peterson
Printed in the United States of America
First Edition

ISBN 979-8-9910280-0-4

Cover art: freepik.com

First Printing, 2024

For the little girl who dreamed a
world that only she had known:
I've found you once again with pen,
and I'm grateful you are home.

Contents

Introduction   xi

Section 1
❧Tears☙

Tears	5
Lost	6
Everywhere and Nowhere	7
Irreconcilable Differences	8
Message in a Bottle	10
Scars	11
Duplicity	12
A Sea of Choices	13
Choose to Fight	14
Through Your Old Eyes	16
Watching the Geese	17
Today	18
Back to Me	21

Section 2
❧Enough☙

Enough	25
Look at Me	28
Which You Are You?	29
Sometimes Words Escape Me	31
Silence	33
Leap of Faith	34
Changes	36
Just You Wait	37
Look in the Mirror	38

Water	40
Intuition	43
For What It's Worth	44
Worth the Fight	45

Section 3
ᨐBack in the Ringᨑ

Back in the Ring	49
Worth the Wait	51
The Meaning of Life	52
One Awful Day	53
If Heaven Is Real	59
The Climb	60
Only One Me	62
The Battle with Fear	64
Fear	66
A Simple, Calming Universe	68
Mistakes	70
Resting by the River	71
Grounding in the Spring	72
Balance Beam	74
The Real World	76

Section 4
ᨐTrue to Meᨑ

True to Me	81
Summer's Retreat	83
A Trip Back Home	85
No Hair, Don't Care (*Anymore*)	88
Unconventional Beauty	90
Taste of Magic	91
Love, Profound	93

The Currency of Love	95
Finding Faith	97
The Dance of Faith	99
Learning Forgiveness	101
Silent Bravery	102
Noticing Beauty	103
Perfect Imperfection	104
An Indelible Love Story	106
Fairy-Tale You	108
The Girl Next Door	110
The Encore	112
Set Free	114
Finding Home	116
Special Thanks	119
Citations & References	121
About the Author	123

Introduction

With any journey, one usually wants to be prepared for what lies ahead. You pack your bags, secure your valuables, make the necessary arrangements for your planned absence (usually in the form of a vague out-of-office email, or securing some type of childcare), and start out on your adventure with buoyant optimism for what your trip might have in store. You also typically have some idea of when you'll be returning home. However, when the journey you embark upon is not one with a physical destination, you can hardly expect to be prepared in these ways. The type of journey I'm speaking of is an internal spiritual journey, one that mimics the same turbulence you experience on an airplane, one that can be just as treacherous as a black diamond slope when all you've ever tried are beginner levels. These types of self-discovery journeys look different for everyone, but they are almost never planned. They are thrust upon the soul, much like being shoved from a Cessna at 15,000 feet on a high-altitude jump (something you will never see me consciously choose to do in this lifetime). Suffice it to say, I didn't plan for this journey. I didn't have time to pack my bags—I didn't even know I had a boarding pass. I had no idea where I was going or when I'd be back. But let me start at the beginning . . .

I have always loved writing, ever since I was a little girl creating stories for my dolls to act out. I gave them plotlines and feelings, families and dreams. I created the world in which they were cast, even at the tender age of seven. My love of writing expanded into poetry when

I became a teenager, when I spent hours writing in my journal, pining for love and romance, and discovering the realities of a world that I was just beginning to wake up to but still didn't fully understand. Throughout my twenties, I continued to stretch and grow my skills, finally believing in my talents and allowing my creative muse the free rein to help me build and imagine what I had dreamed of doing since I was a child. I was thrilled with who I was becoming.

Unfortunately, the universe had other plans for my life at that juncture, and things changed drastically with a massive upheaval in my personal and living circumstances that made me put my writing on hold in order to deal with the "real world." I changed jobs. I lost friends. I moved across town. I began an entirely different lifestyle, one that threw me completely out of my normal routine and creativity practices. I promised myself that I would someday soon return to writing after I had sorted things out. But "someday soon" became a year. Then two. Then ten. It was as if the universe had plucked me from one part of my life and placed me down Google Street View-style into an entirely different set of circumstances to see if I could find my way back to what I loved to do. I'm sorry to say, I didn't pass the test. While I was grateful that I had overcome the obstacles I'd been presented with ten years ago and happy with where I was, I now had children, new responsibilities, and a million other excuses to keep me from writing—and I let them. In that time of creative stagnancy, I had forgotten how integral writing was for my soul. I told myself that I simply needed more time.

Then . . . another upheaval. This time, in the form of a personal loss.

In June of 2022, my father was diagnosed with stage 4 lung cancer. My dad and I were extremely close—he was not just my father but also my constant protector, pillar of strength and hope, who always wanted to give the very best that life had to offer to his daughter, if he had the means. The year leading up to his death was filled with anxiety that I routinely pushed aside in order to become the new solid pillar of optimism for not only him but also myself, knowing he would soon no longer be around to uphold it. Even with the forecast of a fatal diagnosis—knowing that I was going to eventually lose him—his death ended up unseating a deep-rooted fear that I had spent years, if not my whole life, avoiding: the fear of losing an important loved one. The depth of the grief that followed shocked me. I thought I'd been prepared for the loss of his presence in my life, but I was suddenly left adrift in the world, feeling very much like a child lost in a department store: scared, alone, and confused. But I was not a child. I was an adult in my late thirties, with children—a family—depending on me to continue upholding our daily routines, to continue to be the pillar of strength and optimism that I had become, to navigate myself through my grief within the complexity of a world that was moving ever onward, and yet . . . I still felt lost. I still felt confused. And I still felt very, very much alone.

I found myself yearning to turn back to what had once been an old constant in my life: writing. Words were still something that didn't leave me feeling quite so alone. In the wake of losing such an important presence in my life, which was, essentially, my greatest fear, I was left with a multitude of emotions that were clawing to break free. Fears, anxieties, insecurities—all of them hastened to the forefront of my consciousness, and I found that through the medium of writing I was able to better navigate their meaning and therefore process them. I poured every emotion I had within me out onto the pages of my notebooks: grief, low self-esteem, anxiety, fear, appreciation, love. I started writing poems that practically fell from my hand onto the page, realizing that while doing so, I was returning to the very root of my soul. It felt like coming home after a very long and tiring trip away: familiar, comforting, and most of all, healing.

While the process of unknowingly losing sight of my life's purpose began a decade before my father's passing, it ultimately took losing his presence in my life—and the overwhelming grief that followed—to pick me back up and set me back on track to where I was meant to travel all along.

What follows in these pages is a collection of poetry and short prose that covers four main themes that I encountered during my healing journey back home to self: grief, self-worth, self-empowerment, and self-love. These are vulnerable, raw, and deeply personal pieces that expose parts of me and what I went through, but by sharing them I hope to shine a light on the importance of emotional processing in the wake of sorrow, as well as give hope to the reader that there are still magic and healing to be found when one finds themselves thrust unceremoniously out the Cessna door onto a self-discovery journey such as this, no matter what precipitated it.

While the catalyst for my journey was a significant loss in my life—one that can never be replaced—the outcome of it has brought the greatest gift I could ever hope to receive: I've remembered what I'm here for. I've remembered my passion. I have finally found my way home. And I can't think of anything a father could wish for his daughter to have in life more meaningful than that.

Finding Home

Section 1
❧Tears☙

—Tears—

I am full to the brim. Empty of any more space.
Overflowing tears that burn and singe my face.
Worn down by worry. Worn down by thinking.
The waves keep on coming and the dinghy is sinking.
Sinking and falling to fathoms below.
All of it crumbling with nowhere to go.
My feet are heavy with anger and dread.
The whirlpool of thoughts overflow in my head.
Buried at sea sounds peaceful to some,
But to me it is lonely, empty, and glum.
Floating in darkness, no more calls, no more song . . .
Only silence to greet me where I'll soon belong.
I am scared of the silence that seeps in my ears,
Up my nose, down my throat—it all tastes like tears.
My very own tears of my own design
Were the very same tears that couldn't help me in time.

–Lost–

I don't want to but I have to.
I can't feel but I still do.
I'm torn to pieces but holding on.
I'm falling apart while moving on.
Sleep runs away from me but I still dream.
I put the phone down but still look at the screen.
I really need help with no one to ask.
I can't even do any menial tasks.
I'm broken and beaten but still trying to stand.
I am lost in a dark and dispirited land.

–Everywhere and Nowhere–

I'm exhausted and drained and sad, and I feel guilty for being all of those things and for not being enough of others. I need comfort but also space. I need quiet but also normalcy. I feel immense pressure to do things but no will or gumption to do anything. This month has been the hardest on me mentally by far, and I didn't see it coming. I want to enjoy the holidays, but I also don't want to think about anything. I need a hug but don't want any company, but also I'm lonely and could use support, but I don't want anyone to watch me cry. I want to ask for help, but I don't know what that is or what it looks like, and I also want to do this on my own. I want words of comfort but not advice right now. I want to know I'm still loved and cared for and cherished even in my darkness, but also leave me alone. I feel ignored even though I know I'm not being ignored. I want to laugh at the irony of this entire page, and yet it isn't funny. I am everywhere and nowhere all at once.

–Irreconcilable Differences–

I'm tired. I'm exhausted.
    I'm ready to give in.
        I'm restless and impatient.
            I can't wait to begin.

I'm confused, and I'm lost.
    I'm up and down like waves.
        But then I'm steady, and I'm calm,
            And I am peaceful in my ways.

I'm angry, and I'm hurt,
    And I feel like I could cry.
        Then I'm happy and content,
            And I'm left to wonder why.

I am grateful and accepting,
    But no thanks, I've had enough.
        When will this be over?
            Doesn't matter, 'cause I'm tough.

But no, I'm not. Not really.
    Or am I? Who's to say?
        The peaks are high and lovely,
            But those lows sure like to stay.

This isn't me. Has never been.
    I am stronger on my own.
        I can take them. Let me break them:
            The doors to the unknown.

They open, then they close,
    And I try them once again.
        I should give up, 'cause now they're locked.
            I turn away, but then . . .

The whisper of a song
    Leaks through, and I begin to sing.
        And suddenly the once locked doors
            Are nothing more than wings.

It was easy once I realized
    That all I had to do
        Was just keep floating on the waves
            And learn to watch the view.

–Message in a Bottle–

She is confused. A soul who is lost and wandering the forest, searching endlessly for where the path disappeared into the undergrowth. She has taken her machete to the tangled mess, hacked at it for days—weeks on end—but there is no opening. The brambles crowd back in as if they can sense her hopeful progress. They tangle at her feet, ready to trip her further into nothingness, to let the vines wrap themselves around her throat once and for all and silence her cries for help. The thorns pierce her skin, bleeding her faith as she struggles onward. One more hack. One more branch eradicated. Another, and another. But they keep growing back as quickly as she downs them. Desperate, she stops to catch her breath, but in so doing, the darkness catches up with her, and now she is blind. She swings out wildly, hearing the knife slice through unpopulated air. It hits nothing. It downs nothing. And nothing begins to win.

The handle of her weapon slips in her grip. She can't see, she can't hear. She can only feel. She takes a step, reaching forward with her toe until she touches another vine. She raises her hand, ready to clear the path, but . . . too late. The vine wraps around her ankle, grows up her leg, binds her arms to her sides—an ever-constricting straitjacket. With a final thud, the machete hits the ground as she is dragged down with it . . .

And she is lost.

This is her message in a bottle, set afloat on a stream of ether. Carried by the waves of darkness, the bottle contains a light that flickers ominously. Its time is measured until the nothingness catches up with her once more.

-Scars-

I have a scar on my hand from November.
I don't know how it got there—can't remember.
It probably hurt when I got it, but then—
It seems that for healing, only time's been my friend.
The pain from a wound feels fresh at the start,
Specifically when that wound's in the heart.
It's jagged and raw—makes you want to hide
From the rest of the world, staying curled up inside.
But staying inside doesn't do any good,
'Specially when pain is so misunderstood.
But as for the scar that I have on my hand,
How it got there, I still don't quite understand.

—Duplicity—

Where do I begin?
    And how do I explain
        How the workings of my mind
            Are driving me insane?
                All I try to do
                    Is live from day to day,
                      And yet these thoughts are
                      mad'ning—
                      As one will never stay.
What would happen if
    My world began to fall
        With every step I took
             Along this teetering stone wall?
                And what's beyond?
                    Would I dare to go ahead?
                        Would I listen to my heart?
                          Or my troubled mind instead?

−A Sea of Choices−

What am I, who am I, where should I be?
It feels like I'm pitched on the waves of the sea.
Standing, just barely, straddled across
An ever-widening, deep, and dangerous crevasse.
I can't tear in two, so which way do I roll?
Both sides look alike with their grassy green knolls.
But the one on this side I've already seen,
And I'm sorry to say that it's not always green.
The other looks safer, but what if I'm wrong?
What if I get there and I don't belong?
What if I choose the left way instead,
Thinking the right way was wrong in my head?
So instead, I still balance, ready to flee
To one side or the other, based on the sea.
The sea . . . the sea—that can easily drown.
The sea . . . the sea—that can turn ships around
And deliver them safely to a new port of call.
But then, once you're there, you must be willing to fall.
To fall with no netting, to fall without choice,
To let the waves take you and give up your voice.
To continue the journey no matter the end?
Or to give up, weigh anchor, and continue to bend
At the will of the storms that you've sailed all before?
Or to let the stars guide you to a different new shore?

–Choose to Fight–

Breaking news: It's all too much.
The pieces of my heart refuse to touch.
Boot straps on. Helmet tucked.
But I feel like I've run out of luck.

> She's tired, Boss. She's losing hope.
> Make a preserver so she can float.
> Kick your legs! Knees up high!
> Spread your wings and learn to fly!

Back down again. What is this shit?
Who knew I could take so many hits?
The vest is torn and riddled with holes.
Those boots are muddy, cracked, and old.

> She's sinking, Captain. What should we do?
> Abandon ship and get a clue?
> Or hold the course and see it through?
> The battle will wage on for you

No matter which choice you choose to make.
So choose to right your past mistakes
And march with purpose. You'll get there soon.
Find another song to croon.

> Right foot first and then the left,
> Even though you feel bereft
> And empty. Broken. Even weak.
> Find the ground beneath your feet.

Keep on going! You're almost there!
And remember how you used to care
About what others used to think of you?
Look at you now. Scarred, but brand new.

> So don't give up! You're better than that!
> Who told you that you couldn't fight back?
> It wasn't me. I raised you right.
> So get back up and choose to fight.

And remember all the love you give.
That's why you're here—so you can *live*.

–Through Your Old Eyes–

Losing you meant losing me
In a way I can't describe.
It felt like I had lost my way—
Had stumbled in my stride.
It felt like I might never see
The me you once had loved.
But now I know you never left
And still love me from above.
You've guided me for all my life,
So it was hard to let you go.
But in so doing I have found
Your absence helped me grow.
I'm stronger now than e'er before
And now can truly see
That loving me through your old eyes
Has finally set me free.
I love you, Daddy—I always will,
And I know we'll meet again.
For now I'll strive to make you proud
And live the best life that I can.

–Watching the Geese–

I spied some geese flying high this morn
And wondered where they were going to
And how they could stand the strain
Of flying far and wide.

One strayed south of the group,
Flapping desperately in the other direction.
But he returned after a roundabout circle
Of the field below.

Perhaps he found a resting spot.
But they did not cease their flight.
Instead, they continued on their way
Into orange and pink clouds,

Their arrow pointing toward the heavens
And their destinations alike, for
They knew where they were going to,
And for once, I was jealous.

—Today—

Today I'm not inspired.
Today I'm feeling blue.
Today I feel like I'm too much,
And I can't win with you.

When I look in the mirror,
I don't see what others see.
Today I only see my flaws,
And they have broken me.

Today I don't have confidence.
Today I might just cry,
Soak the pillow with my tears,
And leave the world behind.

Today I can't move forward
Like I always try to do.
Today I'm stuck with memories
And thoughts surrounding you.

Today I'm having trouble
Remembering my strength.
Today is filled with struggle,
Negativity, and angst.

I don't feel much like singing.
I don't want to watch TV.
I don't want to have to think,
'Cause that's what's hurting me.

Today I have no answers.
I'm just letting all this flow
Onto paper from my pen
And trying to let go.

Is that really what I want?
I'm so very much confused.
I'm left in limbo wondering
Which pathway I should choose.

Should I let the matrix win
With my head deep in the sand?
Or should I paint a picture
Of the world within my hands?

'Cause frankly, that sounds better—
Creating my own world.
It sounds a lot like fantasy
When I let my thoughts unfurl.

But maybe that's what helps
Make today a better day,
'Cause today was really tiring
In so many different ways.

Today I changed my viewpoint.
Today I chose to see
That everything we know in life
Is just waiting for the key.

The key to finding peace
And creating our own way
Is to love ourselves completely,
Even when we hate today.

Today I found the strength.
Today I figured it all out.
Today's the day I fell in love
With all my fears and doubts.

Today was really challenging,
But it helped for me to see
That today was just another day
Of loving me for me.

–Back to Me–

There is nothing back behind me
    And nothing up ahead.
And until the darkness turns to dawn,
    I stand alone instead.
This endless swirl of chaos
    Has wracked me long enough,
And even though I'm on my own,
    I'll stand up and be tough.
"Life is but a journey."
    I've heard that every day.
Though when no one else will walk with you,
    Those words are hard to say.
They take the breath straight from my lungs
    And bounce inside my head.
This journey is a lonely one,
    But back to me it's led.

Section 2
⁂Enough⁂

—Enough—

At the time when night is silent
And the dawn begins to break,
I am left alone in stages
'Tween sleeping and awake.
    I am left with my own thoughts
        That tell me I'm not worth the fight.
        They say that I am lousy
        And that I'm never, ever right.
They take the image of a peer
Who I knew long ago,
Who used to say these things to me
In the past. And oh,
    How it reminds me of how
    I never felt "enough"—
    That I was simply only meant
    To be somebody's "stuff"
That wasn't worth taking
Along for the ride,
Or that I couldn't give more—
That I couldn't provide.
    Enough.
        Enough.
            Enough?
                Enough!
No matter how you say it,
That word can be rough.
I've learned now in those dreams
That I do not have to listen,

That they are just my fears
Of unknown "what ifs," "whens,"
    And "hows." But ultimately,
    I had to go within
    To pull my own roots up
    So that I could begin
To see me how I'm seen
When I know what I'm worth—
That I'm here for a reason,
A purpose on Earth.
    And so, if I am,
    Then others are, too.
    Even the ones who
    Hurt and broke you.
I know it is hard
To let go of the past.
We can think ourselves crazy
With what we should have asked
    Or done differently,
    That we made a mistake.
    It's a natural occurrence
    From the choices we make.
Change is inevitable.
We can't stay in the past.
We keep going, keep moving,
Keep fighting our path,
    'Cause we're worth it.
    We remember our course.
    It was gifted right to us
    From invisible force.

So when the night is silent
And of these thoughts, your dreams consist
Remember you are worth it.
You're enough
Because you *exist*.

–Look at Me–

I feel your eyes upon me
Like the pricking of a thorn.
It tears the flesh asunder
So that I can taste your scorn.
    I hear your softer whispers,
    Like a hazy sort of gloom
    In a lazy summer rain,
    As I walk across the room.
I see your smothered smiles
Behind the fences of your hands.
They hide your faces perfectly
But not the ground on which you stand.
    So go ahead and stare at me
    And treat me like a game.
    To you I may be different,
    But to me you're all the same.

—Which You Are You?—

You make me giddy.
You make me weak.
You make me so happy
My eyes start to leak.
    You make me jealous.
    You make me sad.
    You make me wish for
    Things I never had.
        You make me angry.
        You hurt my soul.
        You drained my energy,
        And I lost control.
            You are a fantasy.
            You are a dream.
            You made me realize
            All is not what it seems.
        You don't know me,
        Not anymore.
        You are the one who
        Walked out the door.
    You are the one
    Who I used to tell
    Every last secret to,
    And that's all very well.
But now, you are you,
And I am now me,
And you don't want
What we used to be.

Now, which you are you?
Do you actually know?
Or do you think the **yous**
In this poem will show?
    You don't understand that
    The **yous** I've exposed
    Could very well be
    Simply you in sheep's clothes.
        Which **you** hurts the most?
        Which **you** do you fear?
        If my words are uncomfortable,
        Which **you** did you hear?

–Sometimes Words Escape Me–

Sometimes words escape me.
Sometimes I make them small.
Sometimes I keep them in my head,
Never saying them at all.
I've been chastised in the past
For speaking out of turn.
I've had my words thrown back at me
And forced to feel their burn.
I've been bullied and made fun of.
There were times I used to fear
Even opening my mouth
Because no one'd want to hear
What I thought.
And even if they did,
It would somehow wind up as a joke
Beneath which I was hid.
Many never took the time
To learn me in and out,
And so my words got smaller,
And they took another route.
Nowadays I'm better,
But I still need help sometimes
Allowing my intentions
And authenticity to shine.
I find it easiest to do
When I'm sat with pen in hand,
Emotions flowing freely,
Somehow accessed on demand.
They cover up my notebook,
Spanning page to page.

Finding truth amidst the bars
Of my own mental cage.
I'm stronger now than ever
But still learning my own truth,
Remembering the scars I gained
From others in my youth.
I find now that it's better
When I set my feelings free,
And let the cosmos take them
And shape my words for me.
They're honest and they're real,
And not always held with care,
But if you listen closely,
You'll see my heart in there.
Sometimes words escape me,
But I write them anyway,
Hoping against hope they'll find
Their way to you someday.

—Silence—

What is this silence?
A void without sound?
A space that's not seen
But is heard all around?
A way for all people
To say what they feel?
It doesn't have to be fiction.
It doesn't need to be real.
But still we delve into
Every last corner,
Feeling and reaching
Like some sort of foreigner
Who's dropped in a new world
With no place to go.
How do we handle it?
And how do we know?
The quiet is soothing
When the world is awhirl.
So silence your thinking
And let wisdom unfurl.

–Leap of Faith–

She's standing at the precipice,
Afraid to lose her feet.
The edge looks dark and dreary;
The incline, jagged—steep.
    She's tethered at the collar,
    A choking grip that bites.
    It tries to make her turn around.
    It tries to dim her light.
She fights it as it tugs her back.
She reaches out for help.
The monsters got her once before,
And she recalls their hell.
    She's pulling at the tether now,
    Trying to break free.
    She peers into the distance,
    Waiting for her chance to flee.
The mist is clearing, though,
And she sees a brighter light
That shines across the waters,
Illuminating night.
    The tether senses loss
    And tries to pull her back.
    But she's seen what lies before her,
    And now the rope is cracked
And fraying,
Ripping piece by piece,
Letting her inch closer
To that everlasting peace.

Her toes upon the threshold,
She takes a steady breath,
Then flings the chains aside,
And now she's headed west—
Into the setting sun,
Her heart her only guide
As she jumps into the surf . . .
And heads for the other side.

—Changes—

Right now, I'm battling a few head games within myself that make it hard to see the light at the end of the tunnel. I know I'm strong. I know I can be resilient. I know I can try my best and work through my misgivings. Sometimes, it's what I don't know that I find most unsettling. To be brave in the face of uncertainty has never been one of my strengths. I like my safe, warm blankets. I stay in the room I'm familiar with. I curl my toes at the threshold so they don't trip me into the unknown. I close my eyes for fear of falling.

But the one truth of the world is Change. Safety and security are both illusions. Warm blankets are soothing, but they don't provide protection. The familiar room is wonderful, but the world will drive you out. Change is Life's one true constant; one of the few things we can actually count on happening.

The truth of the world is Change. Regardless of our desires, the world will force change on us. Occasionally those changes will hurt us . . . but that hurt is what causes us to grow. To become better humans. To adapt and to learn.

The truth of the world is Change. So do not curl your toes at the threshold. Do not close your eyes and fear the fall. Open your eyes . . .

. . . and *leap*.

–Just You Wait–

The day was dark and dreary,
And rain spit from the sky.
I was sad and weary,
And I asked my angels why
I felt so lost and hopeless.
They whispered in my ear
That it was time to focus
And eliminate my fears.
I asked them, "What's the point?"
And they laughed a little then.
They said that this was just the joint
Of one beginning to an end.
I shook my head, afraid to see,
But they lifted up my chin
And revealed the truth they'd hid from me
And said: "It lies within."
I asked then, "What am I good for?"
And they showed me with the birds
That flew as if from in my core
That it was simply: "Words."
I told them I couldn't possibly be
Of use to make a change.
But what they whispered next to me
Was enough to rearrange
My thoughts, for they knew there was more
To the story of my fate.
I asked what I was meant for,
And they told me, "Just you wait."

–Look in the Mirror–

Look in the mirror. What do you see?
'Cause I see a light shining brightly at me.
Do you see how your eyes light up when you smile?
Or do you just see makeup
That's blurred for a while?
Do you hear the words that come from your lips?
Or do you swear you're not perfect
Because of your hips,
Or your belly, or maybe your thighs?
Perhaps you should see you from some other eyes.
'Cause you're pretty perfect
In those eyes, you know?
Those eyes have seen you learning to grow.
They've seen you stumble and fall all before,
And they've seen you pick yourself up off the floor.
I mean, have you seen you?
You're so gosh darn cute.
Or have you just been trying to live life on mute
And listen to only the words in your head?
Because those are the words that'll beat you. Instead,
You should listen with new ears,
The ones that can hear
All the sweet connotations you say to your peers
But not to yourself. Turn the mic back around
And listen to your own voice on surround.

I am the mirror. What do you see?
Do you think my life's all it's cracked up to be?
'Cause it's not. It's been tainted and rough.
I have a backstory that's seen quite enough.
My glass has been faded, foggy, and cracked—
Tarnished with burdens that break others' backs.
But still, now I shine: polished up, framed in gold,
Brimming with new light to shine for the world.
Now I own my presence. I know what I'm worth,
And anything less will not serve me on Earth.
I am the mirror of a king, queen, or page
Who has finally begun to open their cage
And learn how to fix a cracked looking glass,
How to burnish it up so it shines now with class,
And has learned how to choose
Now which path to take.
The road less traveled is the best way to make
Your own path, your own destiny,
Your own way in life;
To never let go—to continue to fight
Back the doubts and the worries and also your fears;
To know your own worth
If you just look in the mirror.

–Water–

I feel better next to water.
But why, I do not know.
I suppose it must be something
About how the water flows.
I give my thoughts to water:
Let it take them far away
And heal my crowded mind
That always has so much to say.
It's quiet next to water,
Whether ocean, river, creek—
My inner chatter stops,
And I am left to hear the peak
Of silence—freedom from my dread,
Freedom from a boisterous world
That's all inside my head.
It's calming and relaxing,
Rejuvenating time,
Letting me reprogram all these
Swirling thoughts of mine.
Perhaps I come from water.
I move with gentle grace,
Racing over rocks and hills
To reach a calmer space.
The type of water that I am
Depends on where you look;
I could be a stormy ocean
Or a babbling little brook.
But either way, I'm water.
I flow with gravity.
I follow certain patterns,

But they do not control me.
I can be the very element that
Can quench a raging thirst.
I can also be your downfall
If you're not careful first.
I'm powerful and soothing;
I'm quiet, and I'm strong.
Put me over heat; I boil.
Turn it off; the boil's gone.
Without me you are helpless,
And with me you forget
How very much I'm needed
Until dehydration sets.
But I am always flowing.
I'm there for every weed.
I am just like water.
But what does water need?
Water needs direction—
As in, where the water goes.
Take the ocean without tiding:
There's no more ebb and flow,
Just waterlogged wet beaches,
Or else dry, like desert sand.
Without direction there's no way
For water to reach land.
Water needs protection
From the filth that humans bring,
Making puddles full of mud
Out of crystal-clear blue springs.
When water's unprotected,
It gets used up with greed
By people who no longer think
That water's still a basic need.

Noelle Peterson

I am just like water.
I am needed. I am pure.
And as I sit here by the ocean—
Next to water—I am cured.
The waves lap softly on the sand
The tide comes rolling in,
Reminding me that from the water,
New chapters can begin.
Perhaps I come from water—
Ever moving forth and on,
Changing with the moon above
Or rushing through 'til dawn;
Burbling on my weary path
From mountain to the sea,
Gathering the thoughts I gave
To make them more like me.
Water cleanses everything,
Just like tears that overflow.
I feel better next to water.
And why—I guess we know.

—Intuition—

You want to know why you're unhappy?
Emotions swinging left to right?
    It's because your intuition
    Is what you choose to fight.
That deep-inside gut feeling—
That whisper in your ear
    That tells you where you ought to go
    If you'd just let go of fear.
It doesn't follow logic.
On paper it looks daft,
    Like a writer who is struggling
    To finish their first draft.
It's messy, and it's daunting.
It takes a lot of work.
    But the outline of the story
    Is its own redeeming perk.
So what does a writer do
When they don't know where to go?
    They just continue writing . . .
    Trust the process, let it flow,
And listen to the words they write
As they tumble from their hand.
    Intuition's just the same as this,
    Though it's hard to understand.
So let the story take you
And dream of what comes next.
    Let your intuition guide you,
    For it always knows what's best.

–For What It's Worth–

I know you're hurting. I know you're struggling to see that light at the end of the tunnel. I know how hard you've worked on yourself. You are worthy, my dear. You *are*. Healing isn't linear. This type of journey isn't for the faint of heart.

It is hard. It is humbling. It is *raw*.

At the end of the day, we are all our own worst enemies, our own worst critics, our own inner demons. We struggle to see our own value and sense of worth. We struggle to see our own potential and divine strength.

I know you are struggling today. But you are so very brave for stripping yourself bare, for showcasing your own vulnerability, and for striving to release these fears and insecurities once and for all. You are stronger than you think, my love. You are even more capable than you know.

Please keep going. Do not let others' perceptions of a harsh and dispirited world dampen your beautiful, shining spirit. You are worthy. You are worthy of so much more than you could ever dream. And I, your guiding voice, the very heart of who you are, will always be here to remind you of what you can achieve when you allow yourself to **believe** in it.

—Worth the Fight—

Last night I met my demons.
They told me I was fake,
That I should be ashamed
In the mornings when I wake.
Last night I let my demons
Get a hold of me,
And the monstrous words they whispered
Took control of me.
Last night my demons said
That I wasn't worth the fight,
That I should just give up all hope
Of finding my own light.
I woke in tears believing
That what they said was true,
That I was nothing more
Than a bill that was past due.
The demons were relentless
In what they said to me,
And for a moment I was drowning
In the dark and couldn't see.
I couldn't see my progress.
I couldn't see my strength.
I couldn't see the distance
I had traveled from at length.
All I saw was stagnancy,
Impatience, and bad luck.
All I felt was sadness and
How my life was fucked.
My demons danced in circles
All around my head

For the victory they *thought* they'd won
While I lay in my bed.
But they forgot how powerful
My mind can truly be,
And as they danced in their distraction,
I remembered I was **ME**—
A magical umbrella who
Shields others from the rain;
A perfect imperfection
From a past life full of pain;
A beauty in her glory
When she is truly loved
Who turns the winter's barrenness
To spring with golden glove.
I remembered all the magic
That my inner spirit held,
And my demons stopped their dancing,
Realizing they'd been felled.
They tucked their tails between their legs
And turned to take their leave,
Knowing now their lies were ones
I'd ne'er again receive.
I watched them go and thanked them
As they fled into the night,
For in their absence I now knew . . .
       . . . I'm *absolutely* worth the fight.

Section 3
~Back in the Ring~

–Back in the Ring–

When all you want is to get out of the ring,
I want you to remember this one little thing:
That you have come further than you'll ever know,
And sometimes . . . sometimes there's nothing to show.

Not at first. But if you just keep going,
Keep fighting, keep moving, keep learning and growing,
The answers will be there. Your prayers are heard.
And yeah, they may not match up word for word,

But sooner or later you'll see that light.
You'll get to that point where the light shines so bright
That you can't remember those days in the dark.
They'll soon fade away, and you can embark

On a new path, a new life, a new dream to catch.
And that one? That one might just be the match
That sparks a new purpose—a light within you
That burns so brightly the world sees it, too.

And suddenly all will be better than good
Because you believed, and you understood
That life sometimes just goes with the flow,
And we spend all our energy trying to know

All the answers, to be in control.
When it's the moon's timing that makes the waves roll—
Not the stars, not the water, not the wheel of the ship.
So hold on tightly and don't lose your grip.

Let the waves take you along for the ride,
And remember to thank those who stuck by your side—
The ones in your corner who wouldn't let you tap out.
Don't give up now. Remove all your doubt.

You can do this. You've got this. Don't give up hope.
You forgot you already know how to float.
So get back in the ring and go one more round,
And hopefully you'll find that Life is worth being found.

–Worth the Wait–

I'm proud of you, did you know that?
Not sure you've heard me say it.
But I know how hard that choice was,
And I'm proud you finally made it
And learned to rise above the noise.
The world can sometimes take our doubts
And turn the volume up to twelve
Until they've drowned the light all out.
But I promise you, it'll be okay.
Just breathe a little, and think back
To when you thought you'd fought your last
And how you made it through that.
The strength you need and ask for
Resides purely all within.
A bit of trust, yes, even blind,
And watch the new begin.
You're at the threshold, aren't you?
And it's beyond that you can't see.
Don't be afraid, for you've just learned
That you can set your own fears free.
It will all work out. I'm sure of that.
You've dreamt a bigger fate.
Just wait and see, and please believe
That you are surely **worth the wait**.

–The Meaning of Life–

Something is happening. The air is crackling.
The wind whispers secrets that brush by too softly
To hear, "It is happening."
It makes my head heavy and bent with learning.
I awake every day with a deep sense of yearning.
Please, Spirits. Please, Angels. Let this be the day!
Let this be the day that the knowledge will stay,
That it all comes together and strengthens and lengthens
And imparts for . . . ever. Let this be the day that
I understand that we are just aliens walking on land,
That we're here all together for something to learn,
That it's not all about how much we can earn
Or what we accumulate on this path called life.
We're supposed to learn love and forget about strife,
To forgive all the small things as well as the big.
Otherwise we'll never move past this gig.
We're here to learn how to take our time,
To appreciate every soft lyric and rhyme
That speaks to our souls on a whole new level,
To shine up our hearts though they're broken and beveled.
To pass on the lesson of how to finish this mess,
We need only realize how much we are blessed.
You see, every day that you wake is another new chance.
It's your choice to make, but if you get up and dance
Like no one is watching, or twirl in the rain,
You may find that your soul starts to feel less pain.
And isn't it worth it to know what that's like?
Isn't it worth it to live without spite?
Life is too short to live with regret,
So love life instead. You'll enjoy it, I'll bet.

—One Awful Day—

Inspired by Alexander and the Terrible, Horrible,
No Good, Very Bad Day *by Judith Viorst*

It started as a bad day,
A day I couldn't see the light.
It soon became a day where
Every breath was just a fight.
It had every reason
To be a day of woe:
I woke up in a bad mood.
I'd even stubbed my toe
All before I even dressed,
And then I looked outside—
Just my luck! It was raining!
So dark, it looked like night.
My favorite clothes were dirty
And . . . Oh, shoot! Look at the time!
Now I was late: I had to rush
Due to this stupid head of mine!
It escalated quickly just like that
Throughout the day.
And I soon found that
It was terrible, no good . . .
Pretty bad, so to say.

They didn't make my coffee right;
It was bitter and too strong.
Of all the days, why today?
Everything was going wrong!
There was this stupid meeting
For which I was running late,

NOELLE PETERSON

Because the traffic was really trafficking
And . . . nowhere to park. Great.
This was going to be horrible.
It wasn't good. It was NOT okay.
It was beginning to be terrible,
Horrible, and bad in every way.

Everyone was staring when
I walked through the door.
I hadn't put on makeup,
So I looked down at the floor
And found the closest chair
To sit on and slowly disappear,
Hoping no one noticed
How very close I was to tears.
But, as luck would have it,
I was called on nearly first,
And with my thoughts so scattered,
I'd forgotten to rehearse.
So, of course, I said the wrong thing
In exactly the wrong way.
It was really such a terrible,
Going-horribly bad day!

They were out of what I wanted
In the produce aisle.
They told me they'd just sold out
And wouldn't have them for a while.
So I drove across town
And to the other store,
Hoping they would have
What I was looking for,
But they didn't. Of course not.

How could it get worse?
I was beginning to think
I must be evilly cursed
To have wrought such calamity
In every thinkable way.
Things were turning out rotten
On this no-good, awful day.

I got into my car and
Turned the radio on,
And suddenly you were there,
Trapped inside a song,
And I broke down in tears
As I thought of you.
And the next song that played
was also about you.
So I turned off the music,
Feeling sad and depressed,
And wondering what else
Could make this day such a mess.
This day was in chaos
In such a terrible way!
It was a terrible, horrible,
Simply bad kind of day.

I burned a pan at dinner
And broke my favorite mug.
I ate my meal all by myself,
Too shattered for a hug.
I turned off all the lights
And resigned myself to bed,
Hoping that tomorrow
Would be a better day instead.

Noelle Peterson

But could I sleep? No, not at all;
My mind had tricks to play.
And so the story goes
For this horribly bad day.

It sounds silly, doesn't it?
But this is really true:
I used to let the little things
Tell me when I was blue.
But as I lay there thinking of
All the things that went so wrong—
All the traffic and the coffee,
The store and the songs—
And thought about how
I'd let those small, tiny things
Get under my skin
And pluck at my strings,
I decided to think
Of a better tomorrow—
One without bad luck,
Frustration, or sorrow.
I imagined a day where
The weather was bright,
Where the things that I needed
Turned out just right.
I thought about those
Who hurt me in the past,
And instead of resentment,
I simply just asked
That they find what it is
That they desperately need—
That they no longer feel anger,
Or sadness, or greed.

And I asked for myself
That if I could just see
That things aren't always
What they appear to be,
Then maybe tomorrow
Might be a good day,
That it might be less terrible
In a very good sort of way.

You see, your perspective
Is what changes your view—
Not moving to Australia
Or else Timbuktu.
It's changing your mindset
So that you can now see
That you stubbed your toe
Instead of scraping your knees.
The coffee was bitter,
So you threw it out
And had to drink water
To quench a drought.
The meeting you went to,
Even though you were late
And said the wrong things,
Let you learn from your mistakes
And you can take that with you
Wherever you go.
It's a lesson you've learned
To prove you can grow.

Bad days can happen.
They can make us feel sad.
They can make us feel

Terribly, horribly mad.
But everyone has them,
And I'm here to say
That your life's not defined
By just one awful day.

–If Heaven Is Real–

If Heaven is real and I get to see
What my life was like while I was still me,
I'd revisit the times when I was sad
And endeavor to show me how much I still had.
I'd show her the good times, the lows, and the highs,
And tell her that truth always outweighs the lies.
I'd watch her play with the reins of her life
And pick herself up from adversity, strife,
Hardship, and pain. I'd be her applause
In the silence that followed whene'er she paused
So that when she listened, she could still hear
That there was still someone who saw all those fears
That she was able to walk away from.
She lived her life like the moon and the sun:
Shining brightly for any and all who could see
That she was the lighthouse at the end of the sea.
If Heaven is real and I get to go,
What other wonderful things will I know?
Will I see how I maybe made the wrong choice
By continuing to stifle my own little voice?
Or will I be proud of that tiny mistake
That felt, at the time, like a giant earthquake?
Would I see all the roads that I could've forgone
But instead rallied forth with rapier drawn?
Would I see all the people I impossibly touched?
Would I see that I enjoyed life just enough?
If Heaven is real and I get a say
In how I live my life at the end of the day,
The first words I'd want to drift from my tongue
Would be, "Let's do it again, 'cause wow, that was fun!"

–The Climb–

I started at the bottom,
    Where the land was smooth and flat.
        I took my time and paced myself,
            Adding trinkets to my pack.
                The incline started easy,
                      But then rocks got in the way.
                I stumbled over roots and stone.
            I slipped and fell in clay.
           I pricked my finger on a thorn;
Realized I'd skinned my knee.
I hadn't felt it 'til I looked,
    But this trek was exposing me.
        I soldiered on along the trail,
            Stopping when I could
                To see the leaves and branches
                    Swinging in the wood.
                I heard the singing of the birds:
        A distant melody
That guided me along the way,
Though them I couldn't see.
I started getting tired.
    This trail was much too steep.
        I wondered if I should wander on
            Or if I'd gone too deep.
                I was more than halfway there,
                    But it was getting dark.
                The clouds had covered up my view,
        And the obstacles were stark
    Against the dying light.
    They tricked me into thinking

That it wasn't worth the climb,
    And now the sun was sinking.
        I could no longer see as well
            Along this hike I'd started.
                I thought it easier at first,
                      But now I felt downhearted.
                And I struggled to keep moving.
            It took away my breath.
        I pushed myself to keep on going,
    And I forgot to rest.
The pack was now too heavy;
    The scrapes were leaking blood.
        The birds had stopped their singing,
            And my boots were caked in mud.
                But the end was getting nearer,
                    And I could almost see
                The sun was shining at the top,
            Just waiting to show me
        That the view would all be worth it:
    All my strength and time.
And so I kept on going,
    For life is surely worth the climb.

–Only One Me–

"She's too sweet. She's too kind.
Has too innocent of a mind
To take seriously. She's too in her head.
She should see that this world
Is too harsh. But instead,
She just smiles and refuses to look
At all of the ways that life's just not a book."

"I can't stand it. She's weird!
She rubs me the wrong way!
She's too cheerful, too happy,
Too different, I say."

"Have you noticed how she never
Picks up on the joke?
Takes words way too seriously?
Is too filled with hope
That the kindness she preaches
Will someday sink in?"

"I can't wait for the day
That her woes will begin.
She needs to learn that life's out for our asses
And she needs to take off
Those rose-colored sunglasses."

"I hate how she thinks that everything's fine!
How she seems so happy all of the time!"

"And isn't it crazy? How she views life this way?
Her view's just too pure at the end of the day."

These words have been said
About me all my life,
And you're wrong if you think
They don't cut like a knife.
But it's taken me years, even decades, to learn
What **not** to listen to, and how to discern
That those people who think these things about me
Are the ones most troubled in learning to See.
To that end, I pretend not to hear what they say
So that maybe they'll actually stop it someday
And take stock of their own,
Learn to live life like me,
Stop judging others, and simply just be.
Because, if you'll notice, I'm happy this way,
And that's all that matters. I don't care what they say
Behind the closed doors of their mouth-shielding hands,
'Cause their world is not one in which I will stand.
So yes, I'm "too kind," and I'm "sweet as can be,"
But at least I know now
That there's **only one me**.

–The Battle with Fear–

Finding inner strength is hard today. I am reminded *that I still have work to do, and even though I don't expect to be fully healed (as we are constantly healing throughout our lives—we are never "done"), I am discouraged in being faced with lessons I thought I had already conquered. Triggers that I believed were behind me now scurry to the forefront yet again, behaving as if I hadn't already figured out the cause. What plagues me today are feelings of unworthiness. I feel like I've taken so many strides forward and then just turned around and taken a massive leap backward. I am so much stronger than this, and yet I feel so tired of trying to remain confident and sure of myself...*

In my life, I've always been sensitive. I let anxiety and fear rule me far too often. Fear had turned into a character in my life that I'd let take the narrative. Fear whispered in my ear, keeping me from reaching my full potential. I couldn't show myself on social media, because Fear told me that I was ugly, awkward, and uninteresting. Fear kept reminding me that I didn't have perfect teeth, that I didn't look feminine enough, that I wasn't worth the effort of growing into my authentic self. I reflected and searched within myself to figure out just who this Fear was, because *I* certainly wasn't the one saying these things about myself. Fear was every childhood bully I'd encountered growing up. Fear was the woman or man who called me "sir" at the checkout counter in the grocery store. Fear was my teenage crush telling me he liked the pretty girls, not me. But after identifying who Fear was, I realized at some point I'd grown tired of the hold Fear had on my life. So now I challenge it.

I remembered that those wounds are there because I wrote them that way. So now, I write a new narrative: **I am the magician**. I change my own destiny. So therefore, *I win*. I choose to win. I play my cards, and to be honest, I've always had beginner's luck. My wounds and fears will not define my outcome anymore. My faith and belief in myself are the keys to my success. I'm the only one who can truly change how I view life. So, with that in mind, I choose to come out on top. And who else do I want to be, now that I'm the main character in my own life? My feelings of unworthiness do not come from inside me, but outside. I will not bow to Fear any longer . . .

. . .**Fear now bows to me**.

–Fear–

I used to give myself to Fear,
And I sometimes still forget
That I've won these battles
All before, a time or two, and yet
It's still a struggle in my mind
To remember that I'm strong—
That I'm the one who changed my fate,
And I've known it all along.

Fear's the one who hates me,
Not the other way around.
Fear's the one who whispers lies,
But I no longer hear the sound.
I've become much braver
Than I ever used to be.
I have done the work that hurts
But also sets me free.

I have listened to my heart and soul
And kept my face turned north.
I have boxed with Fear and won
By continually pushing forth.
Fear no longer breaks me,
Just throws a punch at me.
And now I simply wait
And let it waste its energy.

Swinging through the air,
Its fists now miss its mark.
With every miss, my flame grows more,

And it can't dim my spark.
A fire's been ignited
In the center of my soul,
And I look Fear into its eyes
And say, "You no longer have control."

We've gone the full eight rounds by now,
And Fear still isn't done.
But future rounds no longer matter
'Cause I've already *won*.

–A Simple, Calming Universe–

Let me take you back to where
You were never bothered—
> That space between where dreams are seen
> And words are felt, not fathered.

The darkness there was soothing,
Not scary nor too vast.
> It's where your mind first went to
> When reckoning the past.

That peaceful, silent waking
Before the light grew loud,
> Before you knew what sunshine was,
> Before you grew too proud

To access these beginning thoughts
That made it easier to See—
> **A simple, calming universe**
> Where you could be set free.

For time did not exist there,
And you came and went at will.
> You built the world you now call home
> With quiet, learnèd skill.

The answers were all there for you,
Within your tiny hand,
> To reach and teach and grow from
> In a loud and broken land.

That space is still within you,
Even now that you've grown old—
> The innocence of youth and wonder,
> Of magic to unfold.

Finding Home

You choose your path as easily
As you choose the books you read,
> The only hindrance being
> Your insatiable need
To see it now, in front of you,
Right this very minute.
> But when Rome was built, they
> Built it slow . . . around you, with you in it.
So remember where your essence goes
To lay its weary head,
> And bring it back to life within:
> To live with you instead.

–Mistakes–

Make no mistake, mistakes I make;
They could eat me up alive.
Our lessons learned are sometimes earned
By faux pas we contrive.
We can regret, or else forget,
But that never helps us long.
We could just hide it all inside,
Denying we were wrong.
But doing so won't help us, though;
More errors we will make.
Until we own our blunders known,
We'll repeat past mistakes.
It happens, Dear; that's why we're here:
To learn from what we do,
To rearrange enough to change
And earn a different view.
When faults take place, don't lose your pace
Amidst the bitter throng.
You can attend to make amends
And choose to right your wrong,
Or you can choose your growth to lose
And repeat cycles, too.
Whatever choice you choose to voice,
That choice begins with you.
So hopefully you soon will see
Mistakes are for the best
So you can start to heal your heart
And rise above the rest.

—Resting by the River—

I rest next to the river and watch the water flow,
Taking along with it all the worries that I know.
They rumble with the rapids, rolling east from me,
Revealing new rocks left unturned
As waters rush to meet the sea.
I wonder as I sit there what new worries will arise,
Watch the water as I wait, and then I realize
That the river is a way for me to
Watch my dreams begin.
I bare my feet and dip them—
No shoes, no socks, just skin.
It's soothing, and it's sacred; surprisingly so sweet—
The feel of flowing fantasies that
Fan around my feet.
The water washes all away—my wretched wariness,
Anger, angst, anxieties: my murky, mindful mess.
And I am rinsed of all regret,
Relaxed and now reborn,
Tricky thoughts left tumbling
In a swirling, streaming storm.
I am grateful for the river as it gains my grievances,
Giving ways to grieve great loss,
Providing new perceivances.
And just like that, the river has
Refreshed my soul anew.
Reckoning the reasons for a rest,
I'm now renewed.

–Grounding in the Spring–

Spring has finally sprung,
And the air is smelling sweet.
I take off my shoes to feel
The grass beneath my feet.
I bathe under the sunshine;
It's warm against my skin,
And I breathe in the perfumed air
Of new chapters to begin.

The weeping cherry blossoms
Swing amidst the breeze.
The promises of buds arise
Atop the hawthorn trees.
The clouds are floating languidly
In Maxfield Parrish blue;
My mind is peaceful; quiet,
As I soak in the view.

The birds are singing softly
To each other in the air;
And as I listen, I become
More and more aware
That the secrets of the universe
Are right in front of me,
And all I really have to do
Is look around and See . . .

To sit within the moment
And listen with my heart—
To know which way this chapter ends

And where the next one starts.
Grounding is imperative
To help you clear your mind.
The earth will whisper secrets
To you, one step at a time.

Together we can find what's lost
And heal the scars they leave
As the winter of our journey
Makes way for new spring's breeze.

–Balance Beam–

I've never had good balance.
I stumble quite a bit.
The balance beam of life has
Always somehow made me trip.

> I've fallen to the left;
> And corrected to the right,
> Taking with me all the weight
> I've added to my life.

It's heavy, and it's brutal
To shift the balance back—
To keep my focus trained
On what's in front and stay on track.

> Then there are added obstacles
> That throw me to the side,
> But carrying the extra burdens
> Won't deter my stride.

So I keep pushing forward,
No longer looking down.
My eyes are pinned on what's ahead,
My balance in my crown.

> The path of life is tricky,
> Not a straight line to be sure,
> But the strength I've gained from trying
> Gives me faith that I'll endure.

With practice, it's now easy
To sidestep what life can throw;
To choose to shoulder one more weight
My balanced mind now knows.

        The trick to gaining balance
        Is to weigh the pros and cons
        Of what my heart can do
        When I've balanced overlong:

To pause and reassess—
Rearrange the weight—
Or continue with momentum
And let movement set my fate.

        The risk is always there—
        The threat that I might fall—
        But I know now how to stick the landing
        And listen to life's call,

To be okay with falling
If that's what happens next,
To keep my faith in knowing
When my body needs a rest,

        And get back on the balance beam
        And finish what I start;
        For the balance that I've learned from life
        Now lives within my heart.

–The Real World–

I've been confused so many times.
    My mind's been up and down.
        My heart has tried to lead with faith . . .
            To shine straight through my crown.
I've had a hard time learning
    To see what I've been shown.
        I've had a hard time listening
            To what I've always known.
The Real World tends to break you;
    Steal the path right from your feet.
        It leaves you feeling lonely,
            Blinding you from those you meet.
It takes the breath straight from you;
    Makes you think, "I must do more."
        It leaves you feeling broken
            On your knees upon the floor.
It breaks your heart to pieces
    And throws them into the flame,
        All the while promising
            The Real World's not to blame.
But then one day, when you awake,
    You somehow realize
        That what you thought was *cruelty*
            Was *growing* in disguise—
A lesson planned from lifetimes
    To see how far you'd go;
        A path your soul set for yourself
            To learn from and to grow:

To find your own way onward,
    Stripped naked and afraid;
        To make you test your strength within
            And see the path you laid.
Every turn and hillock—
    Every stepping stone —
        All were put there for you
            So you'd know you weren't alone.
Illusions can be maddening
    From the Real World's point of view,
        Until you see with your new eyes
            Those illusions were from you:
To test you or to break you?
    Only your heart can decide.
        Be grateful for the lesson
            Or run away and hide?
The choice is yours, my lovely.
    Free will always wins.
        Do you stick with the illusion . . .

        . . . **Or let adventure in?**

Section 4
ಊTrue to Meಊ

−True to Me−

My favorite color's purple
But also blue and green and red
And burgundy and turquoise . . .
But I just say "purple" instead.
    My favorite flower changes
    Every other year,
    But right now I like roses,
    Whose thorns I never fear.
Top singer? That's a tough one.
What kind ya looking for?
I love a world of music.
Good beats, I can't ignore.
    I like all seasons, really,
    But my favorite one is fall
    When, in the sunshine, nature paints
    The greatest portrait of them all.
I take my coffee with more cream
Than anyone I've met.
It must be sweetened without sugar
Or else my doctor gets upset.
    I especially love Christmas
    As far as holidays go,
    And it's something really special
    To see it dressed in snow.
I used to play piano,
But I'm afraid it's been so long
That I'd struggle to remember
How to play my favorite song.

        I don't wear a lot of jewelry,
        But if I had to pick a favorite,
        It'd be between my grandma's ring
        And my silver arm bracelet.
I'm strongest when I'm happy.
I really hate to cry . . .
But it's something that I do a lot,
No matter what I try.
        I hope to someday travel
        And see as much as I can see.
        (Even though it makes me sick,
        It would all be worth it to me.)
I see the good in everything.
I choose to live that way.
I'm told that when I enter rooms,
I brighten people's days.
        I'm assertive when I need to be,
        And I'm also kind of shy;
        But even though I'm quiet,
        There's a lot behind these eyes.
I've always been intuitive,
And it took a bit of time
For me to learn to trust it,
But I love it 'cause it's mine.
        These are things about me
        That make it easier to know
        That I am just a human being
        Who's still learning how to grow
By realizing she's unique
In many different ways.
I'm the one who knows me best,
So true to her I'll stay.

—Summer's Retreat—

Inspired by "Birches" by Robert Frost

Robert Frost once wrote about retreat from the real world, about getting away from reality for a while and then coming back refreshed. His vision of retreat was swinging on a birch tree, climbing to the very top of the tree, holding on with his hands, and kicking off with his feet so that he swung out and the tree set him down on the ground, light as a feather. When we're children, real life consists of a guilelessness that, once we've "grown up," seems to play hide-and-seek for what feels like forever. Now, retreat from the real world seems priceless, though when we were five years old, it was constantly around us. We find new retreats as we age and hope to hold on like hell to that childish naivety.

My vision of retreat is summer, although it began to deteriorate when I was old enough to face the fact that we still have to work through summer instead of play. I sometimes wish I could go back to the summers of my youth when I was five or six years old, swinging on the wooden swing my father had made for me and looking up at the stars that were appearing when the sun was settling below the line of cedars that blockaded our yard. Back to the quarter-sized eyes of innocence, that look of wonder when receiving your first dollar bill and believing you were *rich*, that ear-to-ear grin of satisfaction.

Back to SpaghettiOs for dinner, Playskool roller skates, OshKosh B'Gosh overalls, and Rainbow Brite. Summer nights of running between the trees with bare feet, rolling down the hill of our backyard just to see how dizzy one could get, and throwing a stick in the pool simply because it was something forbidden for unknown reasons for a five-year-old.

I yearn for the simplicity of youth . . . the amount of troubles unknown—real life unknown. Back then, real life was swinging on that swing or hammock, humming "Zip-a-Dee-Doo-Dah" as you made a mud castle with water in the sandbox, jumping in the waterlogged grass after a warm summer rain.

Summer, to me, will always be the smell of grass baked too long in the sun; the refreshing coolness of the breeze that you somehow only feel when under the shelter of a tree; the burning pavement of the driveway that, when five years old, was always daring you to cross it at least once per day. Summer will always be the time when the sunny charm I once possessed comes back again. With it, it brings the carefree laughter of a delighted child who has just learned how to master riding a bike without training wheels; the bewilderment and magic of finding the perfect pebble in the rock garden; and the beauty of swinging on that swing beneath the maple tree, looking up at the stars, and believing wholeheartedly that life is *good*.

−A Trip Back Home−

I took a trip back home today
To revisit my past lives.
I saw the grounds where I used to play,
And it came as a surprise
When I remembered what it was like
To be a teenage girl
Who believed she held a magic
That could manifest a world
In which love was boundless, risky, yet free;
Where a whisper in the night
Became a spell you couldn't see;
Where dancing in the rain meant
She was simply loving life—
Her magic softly sparkling,
Diminishing all strife.
I used to know that girl so well;
Her dreams—they knew no bounds.
She dreamt of love so deep it hurt.
She dreamt of being found.
She **knew** one day her ship would come
And deliver every treasure
That she had ever thought to ask for,
And with it, every pleasure
That she could ever fathom
In her wildest of thoughts—
Not knowing that, in doing so,
She ensured life's gifts were brought.
It's funny—I remember now

Noelle Peterson

How easy it was then
To believe the world was magic.
And now I'm asking, "When
Did I stop believing that
I'm not powerful enough?"
I guess a trip back home
Can bring up a lot of stuff,
Like how easily I used to laugh
And how he said my smile
Reminded him of sunshine.
I guess it's been a while
Since I saw that sparkle
That I swear I used to hold,
Like I somehow just forgot
To "be the warrior, bold."
All the poems I once wrote
Were from a part of me
That I had buried in the past
And forgotten how to see.
So, I guess a trip back home
Can be a message from above
That if you long for life's true magic,
The answer is self-love.
Going back to the years
When you once believed
That true love existed
And was the only air you breathed.
The belief that the world was my oyster? It's true.
Believing's the thing
I've most often forgotten to do.
I took a trip back home today,

And it made me laugh and smile.
And just like that, the sunshine's back . . .

>. . . And I hope it shines for *miles*.

–No Hair, Don't Care (Anymore)–

Growing up, I always had long hair. In high school, it reached my waist. It was chestnut spun with gold, straight, thick, and lustrous. I was recognized by and *known* for my hair, even by underclassmen. By the time I turned nineteen, my hair had begun to thin dramatically, and a mere four years later you could see my scalp showing through on the crown of my head. I spent several years after that chasing ways to make it stay—niacin, vitamin supplements, expensive shampoos, Rogaine. Nothing ever seemed to work, and my hair continued to thin drastically.

After I became a mother, I had hoped that my hair might grow in more consistently, but I was again disappointed. I cut my hair short in a pixie style and used highlights to try and disguise my exposed scalp, but it did little for my self-esteem. As my infants became toddlers, I noticed that I had been refusing to appear in photographs with them out of shame for my appearance. I hated how I looked. I felt like an eighty-year-old man, clinging desperately to the figurative five strands I seemed to have, as if they would finally do their job of making me look and feel feminine again. So, one night, with a bit of liquid courage, I grabbed the electric hair clippers, and I shaved all my remaining hair off in a matter of ten minutes. When I met my reflection in the mirror, I realized how great it felt to have taken back control of my appearance. The effect was jarring. *I actually looked good with shaved hair.* I tilted my face this way and that, admiring myself for the first time in what felt like years.

I was still nervous to appear in public with a shaved head, however, for our society does not tend to favor women with shaved or balding heads. I was called "sir" more times than I'd care to admit, even while wearing a full face of makeup and a dress. Because of this, I hid under hats or wigs for another year or two while I allowed myself to adjust to the change, but soon found that wigs were not for me; they were itchy, hot, and expensive, and they required more maintenance than I'd expected. I became more comfortable in my own skin over time, and soon family and friends would tell me they hardly recognized me when I DID wear a wig because they'd grown accustomed to how I looked with no hair. That soon gave me the confidence to bare my head whenever I wanted, and I finally started feeling good in my skin again.

Self-confidence and self-esteem can sometimes take decades to achieve, as they did in my case. Living authentically as we were made to, though, is easy; it's in our very DNA. Hair doesn't, and never did, make me who I am. I am still a joyous, loving person with or without hair. I am seen for the caring and kind soul that I have always been, and my outward appearance has nothing to do with how I approach life, nor does it define me.

–Unconventional Beauty–

I am not a conventional beauty. I do not have long, flowing locks of hair. In fact, I cut it all off. Or, the truth is, my hair abandoned me, making me feel ugly and depressed for over twenty years. I said, "No more am I less than," and I shaved it off, taking back my power. And now I have no hair. **I am still not a conventional beauty.**

I am not a conventional beauty. My skin attacks itself, leaving me scarred and blotchy, poisoning my image further. What goes unseen is the strength I gain from every stripe, every purple scar. My skin tries to weaken me, but I say, "No more am I less than," and I rise above the pain. In this, I am strong. **But I am still not a conventional beauty.**

I am not a conventional beauty. I am thicker than I'd like to be. I am wiggly in places I shouldn't be. Padded, so to say, perhaps against the words I've heard since childhood: "You're too fat to be pretty." My body has given life thrice over, and I honor it by saying, "No more am I less than," and continue to live, turning F-A-T to a new meaning: Fabulous and Talented. **But I am still not a conventional beauty.**

No, I am not a conventional beauty, but instead I am an empress. Magical, spiritual, and even, yes, beautiful. I have power, strength, and life within my less conventional shell. No more am I less a person, a human, a woman. I may not be what you consider beautiful, **but I am beautifully, and unconventionally, *me*.**

—Taste of Magic—

They ask her how she does it:
How she keeps a steady pace,
How she wakes up every morning
With a smile on her face.
>They tell her she is steady,
>That she's beautiful and strong,
>That she could light a fire
>And bring the world along.
>>She hears what they are saying,
>>But she's unsure if she believes
>>In her own brand of magic
>>That lingers when she leaves.

What does magic taste like?
Like cinnamon and spice?
Like apples from the orchard?
And wouldn't it be nice
>To know the secret of
>How she stands alone,
>Dreaming of a deeper love—
>A love she's never known?
>>How exactly does she do it?
>>And why is it so rare?
>>Let us sip from her clear waters,
>>And into her eyes we'll stare

And wait to see if magic
Is all that follows next,
Or if she'll let us inhale
The sweet honey of her breath.

Her lips turn in a smile,
A knowing eyebrow hiked;
And we are left with questions
Of how she lives her life.
        It's really very simple,
        The answer to her guile—
        She lets the truth come forward
        (With a secret little smile
That she knows will drive us crazy),
And she tells it from her heart.
Is this what magic feels like? No . . .
        . . . This is merely just the start.

−Love, Profound−

I live my life through love profound.
    It permeates my world around.
        Like wrapped in fleece, its warmth surrounds,
            And no one understands it.

They think that just because I smile,
    I don't hear their comments pile,
        That I ignore them all the while,
            But they don't know the worst bit.

I hear them almost every time,
    And though I guard this heart of mine,
        It implodes at the cost of dimes,
            And no one seems to care.

I'm gentle, soft, and open-armed,
    And though it looks like my life's charmed,
        It's what's caused my heart most harm,
            And I'm left feeling bare.

It intimidates those not ready for
    A life without a settled score,
        And even though I love them more,
            They cannot hear the sound.

It gets filtered through the stars,
    Traveling as far as Mars,
        Bottled up in stoppered jars,
            To sell a love profound.

Noelle Peterson

I've learned that people just don't like
    To live their lives without a pike
        That they in turn can wield to strike
            A soft heart from above.

So I became my own white knight—
    Defending my own heart with might—
        And still, I choose to shine my light
            And live my life through love.

–The Currency of Love–

Some think that to be happy
Means the champagne-style life,
Where diamonds sparkle on the ears
Of a business owner's wife.
But a privileged existence—
New cars, big house, no bills—
Can also leave you empty
With a heart that feels unfilled.
Happiness—true happiness—
Comes only from within.
We don't get to leave this plane
With any spoils we brought in.
The only things we take with us
When we leave our bodies here
Are the memories we made
With all the loved ones we hold dear.
And that is all we have—
Just our thoughts and love.
Not the clothes upon our back . . .
They're not needed when above.
Here, there are greed and hatred,
Jealousy and spite.
Money makes the world go 'round?
Well, to me, that isn't right.
Love should be our currency,
Kindness and respect,
Giving unto others
When they've had a life's upset,
Showing them there's someone
Who will always bend a knee

When trouble has arisen.
Suddenly we'll all see
That money means so little.
It comes and goes like wind.
What matters most is how we loved
Once the veil begins to thin.
So do what makes you happiest
And make good memories,
For the richness of a fuller heart
Makes for a life at ease.

—Finding Faith—

Finding faith has been a long road for me. I got sidetracked by logic and lost my way. I chose a well-worn path instead of forging the one with overgrowth. All it did was distract me from my own destiny, and it took deep introspection to accept that I needed to turn around and head back to the beginning, where I'd first seen that fork in the road. Now I know what the beaten path looks like. It served me well but now no longer inspires curiosity or creativity. I feel my essence was drained by the still-beautiful but boring view it gave me. Now I hunger for the adventure of the path less traveled. Now I have security in my instincts to let them lead me into abundance. There's a garden full of wonder right around the bend. I can smell the fragrance of the blooming flowers. I can hear the birdsong guiding me to it. My walk has had detours—distractions that have all been for my benefit and for my ultimate betterment as a human being. I am grateful for the process, despite its turbulence. I'm excited to keep going and to see what's yet to come, for I have found faith in myself now and in the creator that I know I am. I would never lead myself into something that I could not handle or that I could not ultimately learn from.

Does that mean everything is or will be easy? Of course not . . . unless I choose to write it that way. I'm a firm believer that everything happens for a reason, and that what we think and what we say gets reflected back to us in some way, shape, or form. If I think things will be hard, then they will be. If I say things are a struggle, they become so.

When I was thirty-four weeks pregnant with my youngest child, I was sent to the labor-and-delivery triage with high blood pressure that resulted in preeclampsia. Because my son had not yet turned head down, I was told I needed an emergency C-section. Immediately my thoughts started to spiral out of control with fear: What if my baby didn't make it? What if there were complications? What if *I* didn't make it?

My mother was in the room with me when I heard the news, and I'm sure she felt the very same fear and anxiety that I went through in that moment. I looked at her with tears in my eyes and said, "Mom, what if I die?"

She looked back at me, and with the quiet strength of a mother trying not to project her own fear back to her child, she simply asked me, "Do you want to die?"

"No!" I said vehemently, and at that she nodded with an air of certainty that I was yet unaware of, before saying, "Then choose not to."

That simple statement nourished my belief that all was going to be well, as odd as it is to say that. Of course, there are always circumstances out of our own control, and this was very much one of those times, but that small conversation gave me enough faith to at least believe that the universe had now heard my wishes: **I choose to live, please.** The rest was left to believing that everything would work out as it was meant to.

–The Dance of Faith–

The dance of faith is hard to learn.
The steps are complicated,
Especially when your feet may burn
And your sense of rhythm dated.
But learning how to trust in faith
When dancing in the dark
Is feeling out a new-set pace
And listening to your heart.

> You'll find that if you twirl too fast,
> Your head will get you dizzy,
> But partnership in faith will last
> And cancel out the tizzy.
> Trusting in your partner's arms,
> You let the music take you.
> Faith brings out your heart's true charm
> And brightens the whole venue.

And when the music shifts again,
It's easy to adapt.
You know now where your feet have been,
And new steps now are mapped.
You cannot dance while in your head—
It doesn't work that way.
You feel the way you're led instead
And dance your thoughts away.

> I've learned to dance with faith by feel
> And let it lead me blind.
> For within faith my heart can heal

And therefore, too, my mind.
So listen to your heartbeat's song
And leave your feet to chance,
'Cause even when you're scared it's wrong,
Your heart knows how to dance.

—Learning Forgiveness—

Forgiveness is something I've never found hard
When it comes to forgiving what someone else marred,
But learning to treat my own self that same way
Has been one thing I'm not very good at, I'd say.
How is it easier to say "It's all right"
To someone who carelessly turned out my light?
But if I am the one who dimmed it too dark,
I am suddenly mad that I lost my own spark
And had to relight it all over again,
But to my own self I can't be a friend?
Forgiving myself for the traumas I caused
Has been the one thing that has left me on pause.
And why do I think that's the way it should be?
If my friend were struggling, could no longer see
The light that's inside them had been snuffed out,
I'd lift up their chin and banish their doubt
By reminding them once and for all it was they
Who held their own power at the end of the day.
We fumble, we stumble, we trip and we fall,
But that doesn't mean we don't still hear the call:
To keep kindness and love and support in our hearts,
And forgiving ourselves is how it all starts.

−Silent Bravery−

A homage to "Fire and Ice" by Robert Frost

Of bravery, I thought I'd known;
    Considered it a song
        That through the acts of love was shown.
            But as for me, those acts unknown.
                As it turned out, I was so wrong—
I hadn't realized
    That silence, too, was also strong,
        And was surprised
             By silent bravery all along.

−Noticing Beauty−

I like to notice beauty in everything I do.
I like to find the silence in the early morning's dew.

I like the colors of the leaves that turn in early fall.
I like to watch them paint the sky and turn into a ball

Of red and orange dipped timidly in yellow.
I try to find the best I can inside of every fellow.

I like to look at buildings constructed long before.
Someday I'd like to see the world and all she has in store.

I take a moment every day to thank my lucky stars
That I am where I'm meant to be, despite the many scars

It took to put me here. For the lessons that I've learned
Throughout my life have been immeasurably earned.

I'm grateful to have had them and grateful, too, to see
That the beauty that I notice . . .
. . . It also lives in me.

–Perfect Imperfection–

I don't think I'm perfect.
I still have flaws, it's true.
I can't turn things to gold
Or even bewitch you.
I sometimes lose my patience.
I'm impulsive, too, at times.
I get cranky when I'm sleepy,
And I'll still say "I'm fine"

Even when I'm not.
I forget to ask for help a lot.
I don't like beer or wine too much,
But I'll happily do shots.
I rely on too much coffee
To get me through the day,
And I oftentimes believe that
I've got nothing good to say.

I only take hot showers.
I have a fear of heights.
I'm shy until I open up.
I absolutely hate to fight.
I dance when no one's watching.
I'll sing a made-up song.
I'm positively weird, you know . . .
And I used to think it wrong

To actually like the little
Parts of me that seem so very flawed;
But now, I like to think that

They're the pieces that you saw
And decided it was still okay
To love a heart that shines
In her perfect imperfection . . .
.... all because it's **mine**.

–An Indelible Love Story–

I am forcing creativity,
And it doesn't serve me well.
Forcing words makes stories awkward,
And it's hard for me to tell
What I had in mind
When paper had first met the pen.
It loses all momentum
And has little impact then.
It's harder to remember
What I'd been thinking of
When sitting down and crafting words
Out of what I love.
If loving comes so easily,
Then why not writing, too?
Why must I always struggle
With what I love to do?
"This makes no sense." "It's horrible."
"I hate every word."
But then it starts to flow . . .
And the message now is heard:
"Keep trying." "Keep writing."
"Keep believing in your heart."
And suddenly I find that the
Story can now start.
The channel has been opened,
And I can freely think.
The rhyme and meter come to me,
And suddenly they sync.
I'm lovingly reminded
By the cosmos high above

That this is what I'm good at
When I proclaim my love
Of writing and forget about the rest.
Writing words comes free to me,
Like taking a deep breath.
I grab my pen and notebook
And suddenly feel better
When I can write what's on my mind—
The simplest of letters.
A gift with words is hard to hold
And even harder now to share,
But by doing so, I hope to find
That it makes one more aware
That words are gifted to us,
And together we can be
The greatest authors of them all:
An indelible love story.

–Fairy-Tale You–

If you haven't noticed,
I don't play by the rules.
I live a life amidst
Fairies and fools,
Wizards and kings,
Dragons and sprites.
It's a fairy-tale world
That I get to write.
I can fly to the heavens,
Be a mermaid at sea;
I can be whoever
I've always wanted to be.
I can push past those limits
That society holds.
I'll create my own world—
Buck the system, break molds.
Apprehension is strong,
But my mind is stronger,
And I won't be held back
For one minute longer.
I know what I want,
And it's hard work to get it.
But me? I'm not backing down,
So forget it.

I'm a princess with swords;
I'm a beast with a rose;
I'm an empress who can finally
See her new clothes.
They're resplendent and shining—
Hard for others to see;
But that's how I made them,
And they only fit me.
I'm a girl in the corner
Making coal into shoes.
I'm a fairy godmother
Turning stars into clues.
I'm a knight on his horse
Riding straight through 'til dawn.
I'm a queen who climbed
Her way up from a pawn.
I believe in the magic
A fairy-tale spins,
And as it turns out,
That's how we all win.
So question the rules
And write them anew,
And believe in the
Magical, **fairy-tale** you.

–The Girl Next Door–

They say the girl next door
Is the hardest one to beat.
She's quiet, unassuming,
And won't step on your feet.
    She's pretty and alluring,
    Eyes downcast—demure.
    She'll watch you in the garden,
    Quietly unsure.
She'll never raise her voice to you;
She'll simply sit and wait,
Patiently assuming
You'll be knocking at her gate.
    But as the story goes,
    She's quite often overlooked.
    She spins her world of fantasies
    By dreaming in her books.
She doesn't pay attention
To the noisy, bustling crowd
That walks along the sidewalk
'Neath her mama's roses, proud.
    Instead, she pines for romance
    Behind the window screen,
    Gazing at the stars at night,
    Unwilling to be seen.
I've been that girl next door before,
And sometimes there's a chance
That she may have caught the eyes of one
Who gave a second glance.

But I prefer to be the one
A beau goes searching for;
To be the one who's learned
Of all the magic that's in store;
To grow within my castle tower
And then devise a way
To break tradition—slay the dragon
By myself—and run away.

    To set my cap, as novels say,
For freedom from within;
To take the reins of my own horse
And race to my own win;
The one who's seen and listened to,
No matter that she's shy;
The one who took the time to grow
Her wings and learned to fly.

    I'm the girl next door no more,
Whose voice still goes unfurled.
I'm the girl who speaks so loud
She's heard across the world.

–The Encore–

I've never liked the spotlight.
It burned too bright for me.
I thought it best to stay backstage
And let the others be.
You see, when we are born,
We are given center stage.
Some will take right to it,
The crowd easy to engage.
On the other side, there's me—
Peeking from behind the curtain,
Afraid of being truly seen,
Extremely nervous and uncertain.
Ever since I was a child,
I've known I had a gift.
It's come in many different forms,
But it's simply to uplift.
I see the hearts of many,
And I give a piece of mine.
I sacrificed my place on stage,
Still believing I had time.
When I was much, much younger,
I learned to block my heart.
Others saw that it was soft,
And they tore it all apart.
I molded myself into
What they wanted all along—
The stagehand or ensemble—
Even when it felt all wrong.
I poured my gift out sparingly
To only those who knew

That inside me was a shining star
Still waiting for her cue.
But at some point, then,
I realized I'd waited much too long.
The lights went out, the curtains closed,
And they never heard my song.
So, back to hardening my heart
Before others got to see
That my number was **the encore**
Just waiting to be freed.
But no one waited for it,
So I hid my gift away
And told myself the show was canceled,
Scheduled for another day.
I lost myself in waiting,
Still sleeping in the dark,
Still longing for the day that
Someone would see my spark.
But then one day I realized
That it was in me all this time,
And I stopped hiding my own gift
And proudly claimed it mine.
And that's when I conceded
That my song was worth the wait,
And those who heard it early
Would be waiting at the gate—
Tickets purchased, popcorn ready,
And the seats all spoken for.
And the premise of the show
Would be the gift of my encore.

–Set Free–

We oftentimes forget
The very reason that we're here.
We fall asleep and listen
As the world is drowned in fear.
Those fears try to convince us
That the sadness and the strife
That we all seem to go through
Are our only choice in life.
But I'm just getting started.
I've only just begun.
Life thinks I'll somehow settle
For the less-than-happy one.
You think it can convince me
That I'm good at staying small?
That just because I keep my seat
Means I can't stand as tall?
I stand when it is called for.
I think, therefore I am.
I may not be a lion,
But I am also not a lamb.
I will not let life make me
Into what *you* can't achieve.
I no longer listen
To the ones who won't believe.
I am fire, *and* I'm water;
I am air, *and* I am earth;
And I have had a purpose to fulfill
Since before birth:
To bring a light into the hearts
Of those who dare to dream,

To lift them up and show
Them that the world's more than it seems,
To let them begin learning
All again that love is real,
To open up their hearts and
Teach them how to heal.
I remember what I'm called for.
I remember who I am.
I am spirit's love incarnate
Holding space for every man,
Every woman, every child,
Every person—young and old.
And my path will be the blueprint,
Worth all its weight in gold.
So don't you try and tell me
That I can't change a thing.
I have more power in my soul
Than those "rules" to which you cling.
I change the rules I want to.
I make life bend to me.
You've forgotten who you were . . .
While I have been ***set free***—
A bird that's left its cage
With a song that few can hear
To show you now that
Nothing's in your way except your fear.

–Finding Home–

It's been a while. How've you been?
I've been all right, I guess . . . but then,
I'm not really sure if that's really the truth.
I've been forgetting the present
And scouring my youth
For patterns of habit that I still seem to carry.
It's been a rough ride, leaving me kind of wary
Of all the new ways for things to go wrong.
And I forgot to remember that I've known all along.
I forgot that I'd already found that new strength—
One that lifted me up from impossible angst
And set me back down on my own wobbly feet.
I forgot that I'd already learned how to beat
Back the demons of my very own mind
And to treat them as if I were legally blind.
So, what do I know? I don't know anymore.
I just know that I wait at one side of a door
That I have the key to. It's right here, in my hand,
And it opens right up to a magical land,
An impossible place for my mind to go,
An impossible world that I want to know—
To know . . . to be in . . . to live a new life,
To vanquish my demons with a shiny new knife—
Strike them down, kill them dead,
And begin a new tale
Of how I kept going when I thought I would fail.
I remembered my power, my own sense of worth.
I remembered the gifts I've been given since birth.
I don't know how it happened,
But I guess that's okay,

I forgot that the answers don't always stay.
I forgot who I am—that I'm actually real.
I forgot to stop logic and to simply just feel.
But I want you to know I refuse to give up.
I'll continue to nurture my gifts, fill my cup,
To learn all I can on this path that I tread,
To soak it all in—let it sink in my head.
For finding yourself can be quite the ride,
But honoring it is what heals the inside.
So, thank you for being so patient with me
While I found my own way back from the sea.
It took a long while for the path to be shown,
But I think I have finally found my way home.

Special Thanks

The life of a writer is often filled with days of drinking endless coffee, late nights spent in hermit mode, hyperfixation on desk organization when inspiration refuses to visit, and waxing poetic (pun intended) about the subject of one's book to just about any human who shows an interest. I am blessed to have the support of some wildly tolerant family and friends without whose patience, enthusiasm, and encouragement I would not be as whole of a person. To those I sent countless poems to; to those who listened with a sympathetic ear; to those who have stood by me, near and far, to witness as I grew my wings: Thank you all for believing in me. It has meant more to me than I could ever find the words to convey.

And to the Muse of Creativity: Thank you for showing me what it is to believe in the truest form of magic. I am eternally grateful for the gift of being *found*.

—Citations & References—

Viorst, Judith, & Cruz, R. *Alexander and the Terrible, Horrible, No Good, Very Bad Day.* New York, NY: Antheneum. 1972.

Frost, Robert. "Birches." In *Mountain Interval.* New York: Holt, 1916.

Frost, Robert. "Fire and Ice." *Harper's Magazine*, December 1920.

–About the Author–

Noelle Peterson identifies herself as a mother, writer, poet, multifaceted soul, and free spirit who has been blessed with a passion for the written word all her life. Born and raised in Western New York, Noelle began writing short stories at the age of seven for her dolls to reenact, eventually moving on to experimenting with poetry by the time she was a teenager and beyond. She has explored her creativity in many different forms over the years, including (but never limiting herself to) cake decorating, cosmetology, painting, and graphic and web design—though she much prefers her creative outlet to be a pen and notebook or laptop, with a cup of coffee on the side (for moral support, of course).

When Noelle is not writing, she enjoys exploring nature with her children, singing along to any and all types of music, cooking, reading, and finding daily magic in the world around her. She currently resides in New York not far from where she grew up, with hopes to someday travel to see and experience as much culture, cuisine, and nature as the world has to offer.

You can find Noelle online at the following:
http://noelle-peterson.com

www.ingramcontent.com/pod-product-compliance
Lightning Source LLC
Chambersburg PA
CBHW051653040426
42446CB00009B/1116